"The Rob Thomas Method™ has been transformational for our business. We recommend Rob to every business owner who wants to achieve consistent profitable growth."
Dan O'Donnell, Vice President, The O'Donnell Company

"Beyond technical competence in your _____ k of people who will propel your success is invaluab_____ _____ to your career. The Rob Thomas Method™ will ensure t_____ you connect with the right people to develop the network you need!"
Roger Joyce, Former Executive Vice President, The Bilco Company

"It's clear Rob Thomas understands that strong, sincere relationships drive success and create win-win results. This book is a must read if you want to understand how long term relationships are built."
Tony Rescigno, Former President and CEO, Greater New Haven Chamber of Commerce

"Rob is a passionate and inspirational professional who practices what he teaches, every day, at every opportunity. He sets a high bar, and is a great example of the benefits of networking with his Rob Thomas Method™."
Gary Rogers, Membership Manager, Eastern Connecticut, Chamber of Commerce

"The concept of networking is to build social capital in business. Rob's outstanding book and his process expands the skill into all aspects of our lives."
Chris Ulbrich, CEO, Ulbrich Stainless Steels and Special Metals

"As a conscious business leader, I believe that networking is essential to success. Rob is a real pro at networking and helping one form those solid relationships."
Larry Bingaman, President and Chief Executive Officer, South Central Connecticut Regional Water Authority

"The world definitely needs this skill!"
Larry Janesky, Founder/CEO, Contractor Nation & Basement Systems Inc.

WHO
DO YOU
NEED TO
MEET?

Rob Thomas
Founder, Networking in Diners® and
Creator of the Rob Thomas Method™ RTM™

Foreword by
Larry Janesky
Founder & CEO –
Connecticut Basement Systems

To My Parents

My mother, Flora M. Thomas, was the social butterfly of our family. Her connections included frequent, spirited telephone conversations with her Kappa Alpha Theta sorority sisters, about the potential in the next wave of upcoming Theta wanna-bes. Most often, those conversations were the precursor to a more intense personal vetting process with each one of them.

In that vetting process, she asked each girl: Where she was from; Where she grew up; and Why she wanted to be a Theta. Their answers told my mother about the quality and sincerity of the candidate. With that, my mother determined whether or not the girl's goals and personality were a good fit for Kappa Alpha Theta. Those same questions are the basis of the F.O.R.M. process I use and teach today in my networking method. Who knew?

My father, Robert H. Thomas, was a speech writer for GE executives, including CEO's Reg Jones and Jack Welch. My father's communications career made him well versed in the intricacies of corporate structure. When I asked his advice on how to initiate a relationship with someone who was several rows above me on the organizational chart, his answer was, "Who is the guy's Go-To person?" What he meant was I needed to find out who that person trusted—who his confidante or "gatekeeper" was, and establish a connection to that person first.

I didn't understand until much later, while working in chambers of commerce what I needed to do, and how to do it. I have since used that advice to create successful and profitable relationships as an employee of businesses and organizations, and now in my own business.

I dedicate this book to my parents, for they instilled in me the skills and talents that underlie my success today.

TABLE OF CONTENTS

ACKNOWLEDGMENTS

Everything I have today is because there are people in my life who saw something valuable in me. My immediate family: my wife Jen, my sons Christopher and Luke support me every day in my goal to become a better man. There is also my extended family, cousins: Todd, Sally, Annie, Jill, Allie, Danny, Paulie and Eric, even Ross and Scott may they rest in peace. There are Aunt Dorothy, my "Big Sis" Sandy, as well as Chip, Missy, Temple, Matt and Tim and Rebecca. Thank you all for being there for me.

I have been inspired, influenced, and supported by many people along the way of this journey. Regardless of how hard I try to list all that have earned a place here, I may forget a few, and ask for that forgiveness in advance.

Although, I went to a prominent school for communications, writing has never been my passion. For that, I have my dear friend, Tanya Detrik, who helped me write this book, so that my thoughts and words are intelligible!

Four years ago, I came up with an idea, but didn't know how to turn it into a business. Thank you Paul Lavoie, my coach, my teacher, my mentor and my friend for your perspective and expertise in guiding me through the process of bringing my idea to life.

One of the most influential people in my journey is my newest advisor, Roger Joyce, who has his place in this book and in my future. You inspire me.

Thank you, Dennis Brown, for asking, "So...Rob, where's your book?' Also, I can't forget Steve Cartier and how our idea of the "Droolers, Floaters and Snivelers" book title actually influenced this one, (leaving the offensive stuff out!).

I need to thank my nicknamed comrades: Squanto, Skare, Norton, Mooseman, Looper, Rooster, Lance, Wazzoo, Frankie Apps, Tony, Chris— Duke of Earle, Hank, Lorenzo, Moulton, Schulkind, McClain, Dan O., BK, Melillo, Wetmore, Happy Pants, Jason, 'Phil Donahue', Big Pete, Papo, Nate Dog, Dishes Dave, Wolverine, TBill, Tyler, WhataboutBob and Willy! You are all great men who consistently bust my chops and keep me humble.

The design aspects of my business were all started by my dear friend Kevin Field, and for that, I will forever be in your debt.

There is, also, the business relationships that support me. The label "vendor" doesn't cut it for this man and his company. Ramon Peralta of Peralta Design started working as my digital design resource. Over time, he has selflessly invested so much extra time, expertise and effort on my behalf that he has become a good friend. He and his team have helped me focus and grow while remaining teachable. As a team, they have taken me to a much higher level of professional visibility. Hopefully, with their involvement in the production of this book, we shall ascend another! Thanks PD team!

I cannot leave out the fabulous people at my chambers of commerce: Tony, Bill, Laura, Nancie, Nell, Jill, Gary, Walter, Sheri, Patricia and June! You are the best! You "get me," and I thank you for that!

The legalities of business can be tricky. I could not do it without my legal team: Win Jr., Win III, Joe and Nicole. You make it simple for me—filing for patents, trademarks, revising agreements and such. Thanks!

I never thought I would ever have and need close relationships with so many banks and bankers! Thanks for the help, guidance and endorsement, Brad, Bobby, Jorge, Tim, Bette-Lou, Al, Joe, Lori, Jeff H., Jeff K., Jim and Pam.

Eagles…there are many of them. Once an Eagle, always an Eagle. I am grateful for the support of these and others who will be with me to the end: Joe, Jeff, Chris L., Jon, Chris M., Tom and John.

Last but certainly not least, my diner "family." It all started with Rena, and grew to include the staff of each diner I frequent. Thank you for all you do. Your service helps me make connections and helps business thrive: Eleni and Virginia, Kostos, Gus and Danielle, Themi and Peter!

The first inkling of this book and my business was born 12 years ago, when I picked up a friend from the train station. We went to a nearby diner for a bite. At that time, he was an employee of Apple, Inc.. He told me he wanted to change jobs within the organization. The job he wanted was a big jump and he couldn't figure out how to get there.

To illustrate his challenge, he creatively laid out the hierarchy of his entire division using sugar and ketchup packets, jelly containers, napkins, forks, and whatever else was on the table. He pointed out the challenge was his position was in the second to bottom row of this tabletop organizational chart. He needed to get to the top two rows, but he only knew a few people in between.

I questioned him at length about the people on the levels in between. That is when the concept of getting to the top person by working your network was born—at a table in a diner.

Thank you, Nuggets. I didn't realize until I went through this process that you were my muse and my driving force. Rest in peace my Brother.

FOREWORD

Who has everything they want in life? Love, money, materials, help, specific information? Other people! We had better be good at finding the right people and building relationships with them! When I read Networking with the *Rob Thomas Method*™ I was excited to have a specific road map for an area where there seems to have been none. I am an introvert, which makes it that much more empowering for me. I want to go out and network now!

I have 400 employees and hundreds of customers. I teach a class called 80/20 where we prioritize the highest value activities. Networking with the *Rob Thomas Method*™ will help you find the highest value relationships. I have some customers who spend millions of dollars a year with us, and those are the ones I want more of. Find the right employees to hire and the right customers who want to do business with you and build relationships with them! Network like a pro!

Another element of networking with the *Rob Thomas Method*™ is that it is a heck of a lot more fun than cold calling! I teach entrepreneurs and salespeople about many things, but not networking! Rob has filled a hole that desperately needed to be filled. People buy from people. They return to buy more. And when something goes wrong, relationships will make all the difference. "I will be buying copies of this book for all my salespeople and dealer support staff and we'll put Rob's methods into practice!"

Larry Janesky
Founder/CEO, Contractor Nation & Basement Systems Inc.

"You simply cannot underestimate how the **relationships** you cultivate through **networking** can help your **career** and **business success**."

INTRODUCTION

It was 1998, the hay day of lifestyle mogul Martha Stewart's popularity. She wanted my boss at Bell Atlantic Mobile to fire me.

A few months earlier, I had met Martha's assistant while networking. The business relationship that ensued helped me win the cell phone contract for the then Martha Stewart Living organization. However, when the setup on Martha's own phone was botched, through no fault of mine, she was on a rampage to get me fired. The assistant who helped me win the contract also came to my rescue. What she did for me ultimately saved my job.

That story may not be one you'd expect to hear about the value of networking, which is exactly why I offered it. You simply cannot underestimate how the relationships you cultivate through networking can help your career and business success.

Understanding the value of business relationships can also guide you to make better choices along your business and career paths. Case in point is my years as an AFLAC insurance sales representative. I worked hard at networking and selling despite the fact that the competition among the 200 agents in my state was fierce. I joined two of the local chambers of commerce and soon discovered that in one of the chambers another AFLAC agent dominated the territory. It was clear after 25 unsuccessful sales calls that his clients were loyal and his business relationships solid. I was not going to break those bonds. I needed to move on and concentrate on finding businesses in another geographical area.

In addition to those lessons, it was not until years later that I realize that the most influential training for my career in sales and networking came from earning my Eagle Scout badge. Scouting is not as popular now as it was then, but those who know it know the challenge, work, value, accomplishments, and prestige the Eagle Scout Badge carries. I earned my badge despite the fact that my parents were emotionally absent, and I lacked the support that would have helped me. Still, I persevered.

The reason that being an Eagle Scout came to support me was it was also how I learned to be civic minded and a leader. Because of that training, from my first involvement in the college ski club and later joining professional organizations, I was not satisfied to simply be a member—I had to be the leader. Each role made me more visible and gave me the opportunity to make connections with the members, building the confidence I lacked.

Still, selling did not come easily to me. My degree is in communications. My father was a writer and I thought that was my path as well. After graduation, I struggled for six unhappy years drafting insurance documents! Fortunately, a smart woman at a career fair encouraged me to pursue sales and sent me on an interview that landed me my first sales job.

Unchained from my desk, I discovered I loved the freedom despite the added stress of making my quotas. It was then that I began using networking as a way to find business, though my boss discouraged me. For some reason, having to sell made me more aggressive, which isn't good for networking. I did it rather badly at networking in the beginning.

My final barrier to success was realizing that my ego was getting in the way of my success. Leaving it behind, I came to understand the importance of humility. A divorce, the death of my parents and other personal challenges were additional teachers.

Humility made me realize I could not make people like me or buy from me. I needed to show genuine interest in them and encourage them, by asking good questions, to talk more openly with me. When they did, my business began to grow. I also discovered if I connected others without expecting anything in return it was a way of "paying it forward."

All of these experiences, and several years of trial, error, and success have informed my process. The last missing piece was having a friend and advisor point out to me something I was too close to recognize. It was that I had a successful, teachable process of networking. The *Rob Thomas Method*™ of Networking was born. Today, through consulting, coaching, and running networking groups, I help others feel more comfortable cultivating successful and more profitable business relationships through networking.

" **Mutual respect** is a necessary ingredient for **successful networking**."

CHAPTER
01

Why Should You Network?

You picked up this book for a reason. Could it be your business or sales efforts aren't producing as much income as you need or would like? Perhaps you know your efforts could produce more if you had a better way to find business. At some point during the life of a business, you need more sales.

Perhaps you are tired of wasting time on fruitless cold calling or meetings with the wrong prospects. Maybe, you finally realize that doing what you've always done will lead to the same outcomes. You have tried networking, but it just doesn't net you any real results. Or, you've always feared or resisted networking and even though you are holding this book in your hands, you are still skeptical.

Are you asking yourself, "Why should I network?" How does more money sound to you? Did you know for example that one solid relationship could double your business overnight? It's possible. It happened to me, and it also saved my career.

You simply can't underestimate the value networking could have to both your bottom line and your career or business.

Networking is the best way to find strong business relationships. It is all about simply talking to other business-minded people to find the ones who mesh with your business values and goals. Yet, networking is an activity that many businesspeople who need more customers and clients for their businesses resist and fear. Even worse, it can be a fruitless waste of time. Success in most anything requires a strategy. Like many goals, focus and intention are key. Some who network treat it like a numbers game. They gather a pile of business cards that they add to their growing pile of faceless names and forgotten intention. This is what I call "throwing a dart" networking. Maybe you will magically score, but typically, you won't. Who has time for that?

Although networking is an essential part of acquiring customers and growing business, most business people don't know how to go about networking to generate profit. I teach people how to network effectively. I have found that even the people who have some success with networking can't tell you how they do it, because they don't have a real process or strategy. I can—because I do.

Still, for most people the mere idea of networking generates sweaty palms, cold feet and overwhelming confusion. It doesn't have to be that way. In fact, you could enjoy it. Networking is fun and interesting for me now because I am successful at it. I love how it has helped me grow my business. It can be the same for you.

I began to enjoy networking after I defined and time-tested a simple, fool-proof method to do it effectively. The foundation principle of the *Rob Thomas Method*™ (RTM™) of networking is that relationships are the lifeline of business, and relationships happen between people. If you do business, you need people. We all need connections, allies, advisors and collaborators. We need people who believe in us. We also need people we can sell to and buy from. Mutual respect is a necessary ingredient for successful networking. Businesspeople who understand this realize that trusted business relationships can become champions for your business.

Whether you are the employee of a corporation, member of an association, or a small business owner, entrepreneur or solo-preneur, networking is the vehicle to connect with the right people—the people with whom you can forge relationships to fuel the engine of your success. This is exactly why you need to know whom you <u>need</u> to meet. Remember, fueling your success means doing the same for others, also. Networking the RTM™ way is NOT a one-way street. It is not learning how to push your agenda, be a "taker" or about getting the other person to buy your product or service. It is learning how to vet your contacts and get to know your connections well enough to create a network of people who care as much about your goals as you do theirs. It's about knowing who you need to meet!

The only way to do it is to do it! How? You encounter people in business daily. You need to see the potential. The RTM™ process of networking is simply taking the time and initiative to discover whether those contacts are the connections that align with your goals, needs, priorities and values.

Are you willing to step a little out of your comfort zone? Are you willing to trust in a process that will help you create strong, lasting relationships that, with nurturing, can mean profit to your business?

Why People Dislike Networking

Growing up, my parents told me, "Don't talk to strangers." You probably heard the same thing. Now that you're in business, you have to talk to strangers, or at least to people you just met or don't know very well. Does merely thinking about it make your "inner-child's" voice scream at you to run for safety? Do your palms get sweaty? When it comes to networking, like anything else you don't know how to do, you are bound to be outside of your comfort zone. You are not alone, in fact, it's logical.

I was not born a natural networker. When I started, it was difficult for me, but I soon realized I could choose to embrace it or not. I found out that I didn't fear networking, I feared failure. I was in sales, and my sales managers told me it would take a lot of time and effort to achieve success by networking. They told me networking was not part of sales, and that I was not going to make any money that way. I proved them wrong.

Networking Versus Selling

True, there is a difference between sales and networking. I see sales as always having a finite goal: you have a product or service you want to sell; you zero in on your prospects (or victims if you use the "Glengarry Glen Ross" approach); you pursue them to convince them to buy from you. If you are successful, they buy, they pay and it's over. It's a transaction. There isn't any real, meaningful exchange. In most cases, neither party has any interest in the other. There is no networking involved. Regardless of the claims some salespeople make about wanting to establish relationships, most often once the initial transaction is completed, they aren't interested in you anymore. They are only in whatever else they can sell you, or the referrals they can get from you. Networking, however, is about getting to know the other person, finding commonalities, synergy and value, and then nurturing the relationship for the long term. It is becoming valuable to others, so that when the time comes, they will remember you. That is the gold at the end of the networking rainbow that can keep paying off.

"It is **becoming valuable to others**, so that when the time comes, **they will remember you**."

The question is— who is a valuable contact that you don't really know, and whom do you need to meet? The RTM™ offers specific steps, tips and tricks that you can learn quickly. You will be amazed at how easy it is! All you need is to be willing to focus on doing the work. I promise you that networking without the RTM™ process means you are working harder than you have to!

❙❙When it comes to wanting to know someone better, there's nothing quite like sitting with them to **break bread together without breaking the bank.**"

CHAPTER 02

Why I Network in Diners—and You Should, Too

Diners, really? Yes, I invite contacts to meet with me at a diner. I try to choose one that is convenient for both of us, and if that isn't possible, we choose one that is convenient for the contact. I know many of the diners in my state of Connecticut, and I am always delighted to add to my list.

Why do I network in diners? First, because I avoid holding networking-focused meetings at the other person's office or place of work. I know if you are a sales professional you are thinking, "Rob, if you meet with them in their offices, you get a read on how they work, what sports teams they like, what recreation they enjoy or organizations they support, and you see their family photos." That is true. However, when people are in their own office environment, their minds never leave the building. They are easily distracted by the piles of work on their desks, or the emails popping up on their computer screens. It seems they are always waiting for an important call and inevitably someone breaks in with a "little" interruption.

Therefore, when you are meeting on their turf, you lose control of the meeting. To be effective you want to maintain the flow of the conversation. You want to fulfill the getting-to- know-you agenda because the meeting process in my method will teach you how to have a meeting that will benefit them as well. Remember, I told you networking is not a one-way street.

Let's face it; meeting one-on-one with someone you don't know can be intimidating. Meeting on common ground helps to equalize the interaction.

Even though the meeting is in no way a competition, it makes sense to eliminate the home court disadvantage for you.

Mostly everyone feels comfortable in a diner. After all, who doesn't like pancakes, big salads or a cheeseburger deluxe? Who doesn't like a bottomless cup of coffee or free drink refills? Who doesn't like the server that treats you like an old friend? At a diner, you don't have to be concerned about the other person's food requirements because there is something on the menu for everyone. When it comes to wanting to know someone better, there's nothing quite like sitting with them to break bread together without breaking the bank.

When you think about it, diners are "America's Original Social Network," no technology required. It is where people of all ages feel comfortable. What better place to forge new relationships?

I do all my networking in diners and I even have a Networking in Diners® division where I bring people together at local diners to meet others and make strategic connections. It works.

❝ ...think of them as adopting a mind-set that encourages you to **focus on the other person first**."

CHAPTER 03 | *Three Secrets of Successful Networking*

There are a few secrets to my method. These are not necessarily new concepts, but they are essential. You can think of them as adopting a mind-set that encourages you to focus on the other person first.

SECRET NUMBER ONE:
Approach Every New Contact as a Potential Friend

One of the RTM™ secrets of successful networking is often one of the most difficult for some people to grasp—let go of selling! Instead, embrace the idea that you are meeting new people with the intention of discovering a new friend. If you relax your agenda and approach every person as a friend you haven't met yet, the conversations you have will be more relaxed.

Not every person you meet with will understand your approach. Many people think a networking-related meeting is the time for a sales pitch. If you break with "business mode" and keep the conversation more relaxed, they might not follow your lead. These are the people who, like a dog with a bone, won't be able to let go of their sales agenda. Don't hold it against them. It may indicate they aren't a good fit for you or your business.

SECRET NUMBER TWO:
Be a Connector

Another secret to successful networking is the goal of connecting people for mutual benefit. My intention while meeting with someone for the first time is to think about others who have something in common or might be interested in the person across the table from me. I like to orchestrate relationships between quality people who may be able to benefit from each other's offerings, expertise, or connections, especially if it can lead to business.

It is exciting when I connect people who might never have otherwise met. Sometimes they cultivate lasting business relationships and can even become friends. I love when that happens. I love when they later tell me, "Thanks Rob. I would never have met [Bill], if it wasn't for you." That makes my week! I see it as providing my value to the universe.

Don't misunderstand, networking is about finding the business relationships that will help drive your business. It's okay to target meeting people you think would be a good fit for your network, but you have to initiate those relationships with a conversation that has substance. I will tell you how to construct those conversations in another chapter.

SECRET NUMBER THREE:
Invest In Other People First

When you start your own business or a new sales job, you need customers or clients. While there are many strategies to acquire them, professional networking is the most effective and successful strategy because you invest time and energy in other people first. If you network the RTM™ way, you consider the other person's needs and goals before you even think about a sales process. Paying it forward is the way to go!

From an early age, as I pursued and achieved my Boy Scout Eagle Badge, I learned about the value of community, relationships, and service. That training inspired me to become a civic-minded adult. I discovered that if my goal is to meet more people and have them know me better, the easiest way is to volunteer and really become involved with different kinds of organizations. Working side by side with people for a common cause is a wonderful way to find like-minded people, because people who volunteer their time already understand the value of giving and relationships.

You have to do the time; you have to do the work. It is an investment, but it is fun to forge relationships by working elbow to elbow for a common cause. The rule is: Put your vocation aside. It is the last conversation you should have. Focus on service. Service before vocation is service above self. What you will find is ultimately service is about self, too, because everyone wins. Are you familiar with the expression, "Givers Gain?" Can your investment in others translate into business? You bet!

" If you have been out **networking**, if you have a **LinkedIn account**, if you have a stack of **business cards**, then you have the **beginnings of a Network**."

CHAPTER 04

Evaluate Your Existing Network of Contacts

Categorize Your Contacts

To begin the process of defining your network with the RTM™ process, you have to identify who your most valuable contacts are. If you have been out networking, if you have a LinkedIn account, if you have a stack of business cards, then you have the beginnings of a network. Here is how you organize those contacts to begin to define your true network, one that will put you on the path to more effective business relationships and a more profitable business.

First, sort your contacts into these groups:

Friends and family

Co-workers

Trusted advisors

Vendors

People you met or are connected to on LinkedIn but don't really know

People you met or are connected to on LinkedIn and know

Let's consider the potential business network value of each group:

Friends and Family

I caution you about including friends and the family in your business endeavors. That is of course unless yours is a family business, in which case you are engaged accordingly anyway.

If not a family business, most people find that mixing family and business isn't a good idea. For now, I suggest you put that category of contacts aside. After you learn my entire process, you may choose to include them.

Co-workers

Including or excluding co-workers will depend on your situation. If you are a non-sales corporate employee, networking with your co-workers can be important. I offer more information on why in Chapter 12, Networking From Within Your Organization.

If you are in the sales department of your organization, your sales co-workers are likely in competition with you. If that is the case, it is best to leave them out.

Trusted Advisors

A trusted advisor can also be a mentor. Regardless, he or she offers guidance and advice. The relationship functions on mutual respect and trust. We don't sell to them and they don't sell to us.

Vendors

If you have vendors, there may be the potential to enjoy mutual benefits from those relationships. You will evaluate them in the next step.

People You Met or Connected to on LinkedIn but Don't Really Know

This group can hold real potential for you after the initial phase of networking. If what you are selling is only relevant to your locale, then you will want to note who fits the geography.

People You Know

This is your most valuable group of contacts. Make sure that you have included anyone who has referred business to you.

Rate Your Connections

You probably can see that the contacts you know are your best candidates for inclusion in your network. For the next step in the RTM™, you need to break down these connections to a list of twenty people. How do you do that? It will take some thought. Review each one and identify his or her potential value by looking for key elements of the relationship.

> To do that, choose 20 of the top people who
>
> Are likely to help you
>
> You are most likely to help
>
> Have referred you, even if it didn't turn into business
>
> Have helped you in the past
>
> You already trust
>
> Are new contacts you really connected with

Choose Your Top 10

When you have your top 20, go through them again and choose 10 of them. How? The key here is to first look for mutually beneficial relationships. That means those people who you helped who have also helped you. After those, if you don't have 10 select people who have referred you, and people who you have referred, think about "Who should be in my network?" Who would you like to engage in exploring a more connected relationship? It's a vetting procedure. You might consider an old colleague from a previous job or organization. You want to use a combination of your history, your gut and your goals to decide whom to include. I promise the process will become easier after you go through the first round of meetings.

> "Networking is the best way to find strong business relationships."

When you have broken down the list to your Top 10, congratulations!

Define Your Network

Now, you will need to rate each one of your Top 10 on a scale of one to four, based on the following criteria

One – New contacts who made the list

Two – Old colleagues or former colleagues and business associates

Three – One-way interaction

> Either you have done more for them, or they have done more for you. The interactions could have led to referrals or introductions, but one of you has put more effort into the relationship.

Four – Mutually beneficial relationships

> You have done as much for them as they have for you. You may be
> thinking that this measure is subjective. You are correct. Actually,
> the whole process is subjective, but you have to start somewhere.
> Generally, a rating of Four indicates that the person understands the
> value of business relationships.

When I consult with people individually, we go over each of their Top 10
and discuss the reasons for the rating. You really have to think about what
makes someone a number Four. I find that the most difficult choices are
differentiating between your number Threes and number Fours. It seems to
be easier to identify when someone is a One.

Don't fret; you really cannot make a serious mistake.

The next step is meeting with each person. Start with your top three. After
you do, it will become clear whether your rating was accurate.

"Preparation for the meeting involves doing **research** on the person you are meeting with."

CHAPTER
05

Meeting Preparation

Once you have set up some meetings, it's time to do a little prep work. This first step will take the most time, but you only have to do it once. The other two steps are ultimately important as well. With a little thought and practice, you will realize and reap their benefits!

Have a Clear Message

This next step in the process may seem almost a side step. In fact, it may seem so obvious that you will want to brush it off or glaze over it; your answer to this question is very important.

"Stories are the answer because they make it easy for us to convey our value."

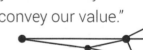

What is your message? By message, I mean what makes you notable or memorable in the minds of the people you sell to or service. Yes, this is part of your marketing, but the ability to express your messages in conversation is one of the foundations of successful networking. It is an issue that I find so many networkers fail to consider, let alone master.

You probably have a rehearsed version of your "elevator speech," but that's not what I am talking about. You need to prepare something to help the other person remember you and connect with your value. How would you stand out in a room full of people who all do what you do?

Stories are the answer because they make it easy for us to convey our value. In addition, an interesting story about how we solved the problem, or helped a client, serve to speak to our value in a way that others can easily understand. Stories are more easily remembered and repeated. They help others understand and make the connection between what we offer and what others need.

For instance, I know a dozen mortgage brokers, but Bill is the expert I always think of and most often refer. He has years of experience and an outstanding record of accomplishment. I always remember the story he told me about how he'd once removed the radiator covers from his own office to lend them to a client so the property in process would pass the mortgage appraisal. (Who knew radiator covers were so important?)

Bill has many stories, and it is a good idea for you to have several of your own "in your pocket," especially if you offer more than one product or service, or you sell to different audiences.

Anybody, Somebody, Nobody

Of all the faux pas and missed opportunities in all of networking, missing this one is the success killer: You must know who you **_NEED_** to meet. Remember, networking is all about making connections. You must have a clear idea of whom you would like to connect with. The real issue is, you must be able to ask for them SPECIFICALLY.

What often happens, and this is what YOU want to avoid, is that I ask the person on the other side of the table, "So, who would be a good connection for you? Who would you like to meet?" They say, "I want to meet anybody who . . ." I tell them, "I don't know Anybody." Sometimes they respond, "I'd like to talk to somebody who . . .." I say, "I don't know Somebody."

You know the adage, "Ask and it is given." Well, it can't happen if you don't

> "What you need to do is ask specifically, so the other person can mentally zero in on their contacts on your behalf."

ask specifically for what you want. Why? Because there are no people named "Anybody or Somebody." If you ask for them, you are bound to end up with connections to "Nobody."

What you need to do is ask specifically, so the other person can mentally zero in on their contacts on your behalf. Then, if they don't know the actual person, they might be able to think of someone else they do know who could perhaps help you make connections to get closer to the person you need to meet.

Let's say you are looking for an introduction to the partner or principal at a local law firm, or you want to meet the human resource manager at a specific company. I might respond, "Well, I may not know either of them, but I do know an attorney who has an office in the same town, or an employee in the HR manager's company. Would that be of interest to you?"

The obvious answer is "Yes!"

Investing your time in preparing a short list of stories (think client testimonials or case study content) that will help convey your value, as well as thinking strategically about whom you would like to be introduced to, will go a long way in making your networking meeting successful.

Do Your Research!

Remember when your teacher, your mother or, like me, your scout leader taught you the value of being prepared? In the case of networking, when you are meeting one-on-one with someone, being prepared keeps you focused, makes the most of the time you spend and gives you the edge. This step in the RTM™ process gives you the agenda for the meeting. You will find others really don't have one; unless of course they confuse getting to know you with selling. We already put that myth to death!

Preparation for the meeting involves doing research on the person you are meeting with. It's a huge waste of your time to simply show up and small talk you way through breakfast or lunch. For the meeting to be of value, you do want to know some key things about them before you meet.

The internet makes this research so easy. You can look at websites; you can Google them. You can check Facebook, but your foremost resource is their LinkedIn profile to see the person's connections. In terms of someone's professional information, LinkedIn alone can give you all you need, but Facebook or other social media outlets might tell you more about leisure time interests.

When you can scan through someone's LinkedIn profile, I guarantee in just two minutes, you will gain some significant information about him or her including mutual connections.

The goal of your research is to identify three different things you did not know, or you think are fascinating, or that you have in common. Write them down and bring them to the meeting.

For example, if you were to do the research on me, you might write down these three things:

- I went to Ithaca College.

- I worked at Walt Disney World.

- I am an Eagle Scout.

As you can see, these three things are not typical of what one would know about me even after a networking coffee chat! As topics, they may only serve to warm up the meeting, but they make impressive icebreakers. What you've done is open the door to discovering the person on the other side of the table. Moreover, we know that people do business with people they like.

When meeting for the first time, that discovery needs to find some common ground.

In the next chapter, I give you the formula for the actual meeting, but for now, there are a few significant things you should know about the importance of doing your research.

First, it can help you determine which of your stories might work best with this person, and after that, who on your wish list this person might know.

Second, you won't struggle for conversation points.

Third, the other person will be impressed and maybe flattered. Because that's also how you feel when you realize that someone has made an effort to find out about you. You take notice because it means he or she is interested in you, not just what you "do."

In fact, it is a good idea to Google yourself and check your own social media profiles to review what others are discovering about you! This is a good time for you to make sure your own social media is a sparkling representation of you!

" The point is, you are trying to **engage** the person in the type of **conversation** that will help you determine whether he or she **fits with your agenda** for building a **profitable network**."

CHAPTER
06

Meeting in Good F.O.R.M.

You've done the research for the meeting. You are ready to go, right? Not yet! Now what? Except for the research, it still seems like this will be the same as any other meeting you've had in the past. What will make this one different? The answer is your F.O.R.M.

A good analogy to the value of F.O.R.M. is comparing it to the time you spend at the gym.

You dress in your workout clothes, drive to your "meeting" with the gym equipment or class. You have your towel and your water bottle in hand. You jump on the machines or take direction from the class instructor, but all your efforts could

"This F.O.R.M. strategy is also a good one when out at a networking event, where you are meeting people without having the luxury of doing any LinkedIn research beforehand."

be for naught if you fail to concentrate on your form. You will gain the most benefit from exercise by making sure your form is correct.

That's when you build the right muscles and stamina. Bad form nets no progress or results.

F.O.R.M. is my acronym and your secret key to your agenda for the meeting. It's not an agenda that you share with the other person; it is one that helps you keep focused on the mission at hand, which is building stronger business connections. This type of F.O.R.M. helps you build your networked relationships. This F.O.R.M. strategy is also a good one when out at a networking event, where you are meeting people without having the luxury of doing any LinkedIn research beforehand.

F.O.R.M. Stands For

"The F.O.R.M. question strategy gives you a roadmap to uncover what each person values and what his or her priorities are."

F.O.R.M. is my acronym for Family, Occupation, Recreation, Money/Message. While these four words don't seem to be indicative of a strategy, they are the makings of one. These four topics of discussion will help you discover points of connection with the other person.

The F.O.R.M. question strategy gives you a roadmap to uncover what each person values and what his or her priorities are. It offers you multiple ways to connect, find commonalities, shared experiences, and interests.

If you are apprehensive, rest assured you will quickly learn how to ask natural and unthreatening questions. In fact, you will quickly discover that your interest will flatter them. When you ask appropriate questions, you will discover information that becomes a basis for determining if there is the potential for a value-added business relationship. Your discussion will also help you in a post-meeting assessment. Actually, the questions make meetings more interesting!

You will find that before long, you will have your own repertoire for all of the F.O.R.M. questions. What I offer are my suggestions and examples.

"When you ask appropriate questions, you will discover information that becomes a basis for determining if there is the potential for a value-added business relationship."

F is for Family

I can almost hear you thinking, how do I ask about family? Do I say, "How's your family?" No! Instead, ask, "Where is home?" To them, home can mean different places, and maybe involve different people and history. Notice the question wasn't, "Where do you live?" Instead, asking, "Where is home?" is a more expansive question. It's friendlier and feels less like an interrogation.

O is for Occupation

It's logical to ask someone you've just met, "What's your business?" or "What do you do for a living?" However, when you are meeting with one of your Top 10 contacts, you probably already know that answer. Rather a better question would be, "I know what you do, but how did you choose that field? How did you end up at your current company?" These are great questions to ask of someone you know, because they expand the conversation to include a wider scope of topics to explore. Perhaps the person will share more of their history, education, and even geography if they have relocated.

You might have gotten some of this information in your research, but there are always stories behind the career that are interesting and could be revealing.

R is for Recreation

Questions about recreation might be the easiest! "What do you do for fun when you're not on the job?" is a good question! Another way to ask is, "What do you do in your free time?" The answers can easily and naturally lead you to explore more from your own curiosity.

M is for Money or Message

If you are thinking it doesn't seem right or logical to ask specifically about the person's money, finances or message, you are right. This F.O.R.M. question has a different strategy. I will begin at the end in order to help you understand the purpose behind asking these next questions, because the questions themselves may puzzle you.

> "What will be most revealing is if he or she actually knows what they really want!"

The unobvious purpose in this section of the F.O.R.M. process is that the person's answers to these questions will help you determine if you want to pursue a stronger connection. Indicators will be how each person views his or her career, what his or her goals are, how invested each is in success, and what motivates them. Finally, you will discover who among them understands the value of networking. What will be most revealing is if he or she actually knows what they really want!

The point is, you are trying to engage the person in the type of conversation that will help you determine whether he or she fits with your agenda for building a profitable network. I am often surprised by the answers I receive, and you may be, too.

What questions can you ask to get to this stage? Questions such as, "What do you want to be when you grow up? Do you like your job? Do you want to do this the rest of your life? What are you are trying to accomplish in this role or phase of your career? What is your secret dream for your life? What's the difference between what you need and what you really want?"

Again, you may be surprised by the variety of answers you will hear. You will learn if the person is confident or struggling, or if something else is dictating his or her life's path.

Examples of answers and what they might mean:

- If I don't make over six figures in the next year, I have to find a second job. - *Motivated*

- I have two kids in college, I have to keep them there. - *Motivated*

- To tell you the truth, I have cancer. I have to keep this position to retain my insurance benefits or feed the family. – *May not have the energy to be invested in networking*

- I am just doing this until I can retire. – *May not be motivated*

- I've always wanted to . . . Could be a great connection, need to know more about why the person hasn't, or what's holding him or her back.

- I don't know. *Red flag.*

- I am doing great. I don't have to network, people just call me. *Forget it!!!*

As the title of this book says, the pivotal question to ask is, "Who do you need to meet?" or, "Who would be a good connection for you." I may know the person you want to connect with, or a person in a company you are interested in meeting with. If they respond with "Anybody . . ." or "Somebody," as I discussed in Chapter 2, this is a red flag! You can prompt them for a more definitive answer by suggesting some names, companies or titles of who they would like to be connected with.

Take Notes

I always take notes, and I recommend that you do, because when you do, this kind of in-depth and continual networking, you won't be able to remember the conversations.

First, I take notes because I want to capture key information about each person. I begin by always writing the word F.O.R.M., down along the side of the page as a reminder to myself of the process I am following.

Second, taking notes communicates that I value their answers, and it demonstrates my commitment to investing in the relationship. If you ask, "Do you mind if I take notes?" it will indicate your sincere interest in them. People like this! You could also say, "I am just jotting down a few things I want to remember about our conversation." Again, I find it seems to flatter them. Ironically, most people don't ask me at all. So I just go ahead and do it anyway!

I use a 5x7 black, leather-covered journal for note taking. It is small enough to carry with me and it is professional looking. Using the notebook, instead of technology makes it more personal, too.

You are finally ready to go!

" That is when I knew that the relationship was going to last and that I could probably ask him for anything.

CHAPTER
07 | *The Meeting*

It's meeting day. You are at the meeting. You have your notebook, with your notes and your F.O.R.M. reminder. From this point on, it is just a friendly conversation.

Build Rapport

A networking coffee or lunch always starts out the same way; you want to "build rapport." When meeting with someone you don't really know, building rapport is something you probably do naturally. It usually involves initial chatter about the weather, the traffic or the place you are meeting.

Positioning

Next, you want to offer a positioning statement. Specifically, this is to verify the purpose for the meeting, so the other person is clearly aware and aligned. You want to say something like, "Chris, I'm glad we made this time to get together. I'd like to know more about you, and see how we might help each other in business."

To start, recap how you both came to be connected. If this person is one of your Top 10, you could also offer, "I remember when I first met you. I can't believe we haven't gotten together like this before."

If it is a first-time meeting, mention how you met. Perhaps you could say, "It was great to meet you at that networking event. What did you think of the event?" Or, if it was a referral, "It was nice of Suzie Que to connect us. I've known her since . . . How are you two connected?" Once you get beyond the rapport and positioning, you can jump right into the F.O.R.M. process.

Your Message, Your Stories, Your Ask

In Chapter 5, I discussed how important it is to be clear about your message and having pre-selected stories that showcase your expertise and value. Hopefully, the other person will be business savvy enough to ask you questions, too. If not, he or she may not be a good connection. If you can, interject what types of businesses you serve and the value you bring. Even if he or she does not seem to be a good connection, being specific about who you need to meet could open up new conversation and give the meeting a more positive outcome.

The Offer

If it has not happened during the meeting, the end of the meeting is a good time to ask who the other person would like to meet, or what company would they like to do business with. This is where you may get the "anybody, somebody" answer. Ask for clarification, if it turns out that you do know someone who would be a good fit, you can decide if you want to make the connection. If you cannot, you can simply say you will keep the request in mind when you are networking. It's your choice!

Here is an example of how I used F.O.R.M. to impress Roger, the executive vice president of a prominent manufacturing firm in Connecticut. He intimidated me. However, I knew that he is a trusted contact within my network. I wanted to get to know him better. How was I going to do that? I sent him an email, and I called him and asked him to lunch. He said, "Sure, Rob. I would love to." I couldn't believe it was so easy. Then, I became really nervous.

I did some LinkedIn research. I wrote my list of three things. Actually, I think at that time I wrote down five things on the back of my business card. I put his name on the top with the date.

The five things I discovered on his LinkedIn profile were intriguing. I was curious about certain aspects of his background that were new to me. I placed the business card next to me while we had lunch. Although I was taking notes in my journal, every so often I would glance at my business   card list.

About midway through lunch, he interjected, "Okay, you have got to stop. Just stop, time out. What is that card? What is on that card that you're reading from on the table? What is that?" Quickly recovering from my silent panic attack, I said, "Well, on the card I wrote the things that I wanted to ask you about. I jotted them down on my card because I wanted to make sure that I gave it to you so that you would remember our meeting."

He said, "Really? Who taught you that?" I told him it was something that I found could help me remember what I wanted to ask him.

He then said, "Rob, this has got to be the most professional, organized, effective lunch meeting I've ever had with anyone in business, ever, and I've been in business for 35 years."

I relaxed as he asked me more about myself, what I was doing and why. We even got into my home life. Then he asked me how he could help me. That is when I knew that the relationship was going to last and that I could probably ask him for anything. If he could not provide it, I knew he would at least give me a resource or his advice on how I could get what I was looking for.

So, that's a testament to doing the research, and asking pertinent questions that help guide the conversation. I used my F.O.R.M. process effectively, and it made all the difference by adding a highly valuable contact to my network.

" Your goal is to determine if the person is a good fit. That is why I created the rating scale. It all comes down to answering the question, **'Is this person the right one to invest my time and effort in?'"**

CHAPTER 08 | *Post Meeting Debriefing*

Assess, Classify, Nurture

Congratulations, for making it to this part of the process because this is where it all comes together. This is the step where you begin to gain traction in creating your value-added business network. Here is where you learn the important process of evaluating the meeting within the context of your goals. You will learn to rate each person for potential inclusion in your network. You do this because your time is valuable. I must repeat, YOUR TIME IS VALUABLE! I often find that so many people forget that. Because they are the ones who are initiating the meetings as the process to build their networks, they seem to forget they also have value to offer as well. You will discover that through the process of being selective, you are honoring your value and your time. Remember, each person is vying for a position in your network and your evolving Top 10. They have to be worthy of the position, because you give as much value as you will receive from it.

Also, realize that I refer to it as your evolving Top 10, because this will be a continuous process. Relationships and circumstances change as you nurture your network. I will tell you more about what nurturing involves later.

It is best to do your post-meeting evaluation as soon after your meeting as possible. Do it immediately if you can. This is where you will be glad you took notes, which will be valuable in your assessment. Your impressions will also assist you in this process.

During this process, you will also discover how you will want to refine your note-taking going forward. If you are following my process from the beginning, your first meetings will be with people you already know. I have found when coaching people in this process, they can discover during debriefing that some of their Top 10 choices turn out to be less valuable than they had believed. That is why your notes and the awareness you gain by working the RTM™ process are so valuable.

In the beginning, debriefing the meeting may challenge your objectivity. This is what the rating scale is for. Please realize, there are no fatal mistakes. The rating scale will help you objectively evaluate your conversations. From examining them, you will be more able to rate each person's value to you. Your goal is to determine if the person is a good fit. That is why I created the rating scale. It all comes down to answering the question, "Is this person the right one to invest my time and effort in?"

The rating helps us be objective. For example, Larry and I met for breakfast. He is a president and CEO of a major company in my area. I want him in my network because of his position. However, I can't force that relationship. It would be great if he emailed me or invited me to meet for coffee or lunch from time to time, but we don't have that kind of a relationship, yet. For now, I have to rate him according to our meeting instead of how I hope it will eventually be. For now, Larry is an "11" on my list.

I haven't addressed what an 11 is but anyone who isn't on my Top 10 list, but with whom I plan to keep in contact with is an 11. I will choose to keep in touch with Larry, even though it wasn't evident how the future value of our relationship might present itself. He is well connected and open to meeting with me, and because in our meeting I discovered something else. It came from a small act of bravery on my part. I asked him a question I wouldn't have typically asked. I said, "Larry, I've got to ask you, is it really lonely at the top?" He didn't hesitate when he responded, "Rob, you have no idea. It really is. People at work are intimidated by my title. I can't go to lunch or breakfast with any of my employees. My direct staff maybe, but any of the line workers, absolutely not. They're scared to death of me."

I would not have dared to ask that question had I not felt the meeting was going well. Because I have a good deal of practice in this process, I felt comfortable in doing so. Like me, you will find that meetings and ratings will become easier over time. Actually, after the meeting I got to thinking about Larry and our conversation. It occurred to me that I knew someone who shared a personal interest of Larry's. I will finish telling the rest of this story in the next section about nurturing your network.

Classifications follow my descriptions in Chapter 4, but now you can apply them to an actual person and meeting. It should all begin to make sense to you now.

"You didn't make them do it; You didn't ask them to do it, they just did it on their own, because they actually care. They cared enough about the conversation and you that they asked about you."

In fact, the more you use the classifications, the more aware you will become of people's behavior as it pertains to networking. For instance, you will inevitably meet those who respond to your F.O.R.M. questions by talking for the entire time about themselves. These people never ask you questions. Even if you are able to interject your message or your "ask", they won't pick up on it. They won't show any interest in you. In the rare occasion they do, you will probably sense an insincerity. They clearly don't understand how business works or thrives. More importantly, they don't understand the art of conversation or the concept of reciprocity. In the networking world of give and take, these people are oblivious. Even if you like them, they will never recommend you or connect you to anyone else. For that reason, they should be off your list, totally.

You will also begin to notice when the other person asks you questions, what kind of questions they are, because the questions will offer you clues as to what kind of networker he or she is. Did he or she reciprocate in asking something equal to your F.O.R.M. questions? If so, that's a good sign. This is the turning point. Organically now, and without provocation, they started asking you about you. You didn't make them do it; You didn't ask them to do it, they just did it on their own, because they actually care. They cared enough about the conversation and you that they asked about you.

"Organic Switch... it's a pivotal indication that the person is interested in making a real connection with you. It shows they value your time and theirs."

I call this sign, the "Organic Switch." It is a pivotal indication that the person is interested in making a real connection with you. It shows they value your time and theirs. It's likely they are good networkers, and as a result, they have many good contacts and connections they will hopefully share with you in the future.

Hopefully, the questions were about your story, more details about you, what you offer your clients, or the connections you are looking for. If the person seemed interested in pursuing the newly created connection, you could consider a rating of Two for that person. If he or she were forthcoming with ideas about people they could connect you with, the rating could be a Two or a Three. If he or she offered a connection to you, or more help than you were able to offer, a Three would be a good rating, and then you have some work to do by including them in your network. If you exchanged connections or planned a next step with that in mind, the rating could even be a Four. If his or her business also works with your target market, that might deserve a rating of Four providing they offer to include you as a resource.

Please relax and remember, you can't make a mistake here. The classification just helps you determine if you want to pursue the relationship. If you plan to include him or her in the list of people with whom you want to keep in touch, how and how often will you do that? What does the process of nurturing your Top 10 list of contacts look like?

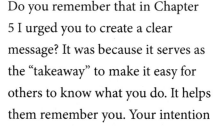

"...a good, old-fashioned handwritten Thank You note"

Do you remember that in Chapter 5 I urged you to create a clear message? It was because it serves as the "takeaway" to make it easy for others to know what you do. It helps them remember you. Your intention is to be remembered as the go-to person in your field. Doing so will set you apart from the competition. That said, I have another secret weapon. There is something more you can do to be memorable—something that will help to differentiate you. That is a Thank You note. Notice, I did not say the thank you email or voicemail. I said "note." I mean a good, old-fashioned handwritten Thank You note. Who writes handwritten notes anymore, you ask? No one. If you've received one in the past few years, what did you do with it? I will bet you didn't throw it out. I bet at some point you've had a handwritten note sitting on your credenza or pinned on your bulletin board. In part because it is nice to receive one, and you didn't want to throw it out. Because we all know the time and effort it takes to write one, put it in an envelope, hand stamp it, and mail it. Also, if you've ever received one, you know it continues to make you feel special every time you look at it. You remember the reason the person sent it, and you remember him or her, too!

Maybe you subscribe to an electronically generated card-sending service. That method can be useful in some situations, but if you want to differentiate yourself, put the electronic production aside for this. Send a handwritten note. I guarantee it will gain you positive recognition. It lets the person know you value his or her time. People tend to remember that.

"The number one key to nurturing your network is following up with a contact."

The final step in the RTM™ is to determine how to continue to nurture your network. You definitely need a process for this and a tool to keep track of it. You are going to build a large network of people. You may remember who your Top 10 people are, though, they will change. However, you will never be able to remember all of your 11s – the people of value who you want to keep as potentials in your network. If you don't have a process in place to keep track of them, you will lose valuable traction. If you don't have a contact management system with a reminder capability, it will become overwhelming and impossible to manage.

There are many choices of contact management systems on the market, from full-blown Customer Resource Management (CRM) software to simple contact management tools like Microsoft Outlook. If you are an Apple user, there is a software called LincSphere that I use. It's free for up to 50 contacts. It's designed specifically for networking. It prompts you to follow-up with contacts. It helps you keep in touch with them, because the whole idea of having a network is to stay connected to them; specifically, your Top 10 list, but also to keep your 11's in the rotation as well.

Whatever method of tracking you choose, you have to have a plan on what keeping in touch means to you. I am often asked, "What do you mean by keeping in touch? What do I do or say, how and when?"

The number one key to nurturing your network is following up with a contact. It is a tried-and-true philosophy in the world of sales— staying "top of mind." The easiest way to do that is to use your meeting notes to remember what the person said. That's another way that taking notes serves you beyond the initial meeting. You can even put some of that information in your contact manager. When you know what is important to your contacts either personally or professionally, you have the makings of things to offer when you want to reach out and say "Hello."

For instance, my videographer loves old cars. When I am driving around, if I spot an old car, I give him a heads up because his passion is to restore old cars. How could I possibly have known that if I hadn't asked when we had lunch? Since then, when I see an old or vintage car, it makes me think of him. As soon as I can, I give him a call or message him to say I thought of him because . . . I describe the car I saw. Then I ask how he's doing and what's going on with him. This can happen via a message or a live phone call. If it is a message, I tell him to give me a call sometime when he's free to do so. Even if he doesn't, I reminded him that he's important to me.

Here's another example. Remember, I told you that after my meeting with Larry, my CEO contact, I realized there was one person in my network that he might be interested in connecting with. I actually remembered that Ramon, another of my contacts, shared a common interest with Larry. Ramon is a successful business owner, who, like Larry, is a Porsche car enthusiast. They own several between them. I connected them by sending this simple email.

> "Larry, meet Ramon. Ramon, meet Larry. I am connecting you because, after having breakfast with Larry this morning, I thought you two might be interested to know that you both love and have Porsche automobiles. I'll let the two of you discover the details, but I thought on both a personal and professional basis, you might enjoy connecting."

I don't know if they will actually connect. If they do, I will bet at some point I will hear about it. Even if they don't, I reached out and touched each of them in a thoughtful, non-sales way. I got my name in front of both of them and demonstrated that I value them by remembering something about them, and I took the time and effort to make that connection in my memory and then between them.

Connecting others in this way is a concept some people just don't understand. For instance, I recounted this story to two of the bankers in one of my Networking in Diners® groups. They could not imagine why I would connect Larry and Ramon. They especially felt they themselves weren't interested in having me connect them to who wasn't poised to do business with them. I told them it was because I am unable to make anyone do business with them or anyone else. All I can do is connect or introduce good people I know. "You know," I said, "when I introduce people, they have the opportunity to ask questions and find out for themselves if there is potential value in the relationship."

As I said, my rating system is a way to approach qualifying potential value. It helps you see and evaluate potential. While Larry isn't on my Top 10 list, I value him. Ramon is on my list, and I made the introduction because they have a common interest. If they take time to have a business conversation that indicates there is additional value there, that's great.

> "It is NOT directly about sales and it's not even about doing business. It's about connecting people who understand the value of connections."

This is an example of nurturing your network. It is NOT directly about sales and it's not even about doing business. It's about connecting people who understand the value of connections.

Also, introductions are so much easier, more plentiful and simpler to do when there is no inference that business is going to occur. There are so many interesting opportunities to pay it forward, just because it feels good.

If during a meeting someone expresses a need, I offer to connect them to others I know that could potentially fill that need. When I do connect them, if I have no personal experience working with them, I simply offer that I know and trust them to be reputable.

For instance, if someone needs insurance because they're buying a home or they fired their insurance agent, I mention that I have several in my network. I offer two or three names, but they have to determine in their own way who is right for them.

Even though I shared this philosophy with the two bank reps, they still did not understand. They thought making connections like Larry and Ramon was just a waste of time. "Okay", I said, "Do you want to just eat some fish today, or do you want to learn how to catch fish and eat for a lifetime?"

That's why I call it nurturing your network. Because ultimately people will do business with people they know and trust. It's what differentiates my process. There are no leads, there are no referrals, there are only introductions. It is the process of encouraging new contacts to meet the good people I know and respect. What happens organically is that the good people prevail in my network.

As I have grown my own network, which is rather large, I've gone from just a Top 10 list to a Top 30 list. I have gone through the process of evaluating my entire list of contacts, some of whom I've known for years. I've rated all of them on the scale according to where they fit for me. I have several 11s and 1,000+ connections on LinkedIn, and I am always adding…and removing :-0

I'm also constantly refining— wash, rinse, and repeat. I periodically review my Top 30. For instance, it initially seemed that my contact Nichole would be good to include. I've since realized that she's not. It wasn't anything particularly negative, but a specific encounter demonstrated that our intentions weren't aligned as I had originally thought. I will keep her on my follow-up list. I'm not erasing her from my network, but she moved down from my Top 30 list to my 11s. My Top 30, like the Top 10 I recommend you start with, are the people who have really shown me they value working with me and are invested in the process of doing business as I am.

That's what the RTM™ process it is all about!

" ...I promise..that all they have to do is **meet one new person**. If they do that, they can go home."

CHAPTER 09

How to Network at a Networking Event

Why would you go to a networking event? Because it is one of the easiest ways to meet the largest number of new people in the shortest amount of time. It is a way to find new people to include in your network. This same potential also exists at seminars or trade shows. The difference is that at a networking event the sole purpose is to meet new people. Trade shows and seminars have different main agendas. At a networking event, everyone is there for one purpose- to meet new people. However, you will always find people who are only comfortable talking with the people they know. I see that as lost opportunities. Connecting with people you know is a part of networking, but this chapter is about how to attend a networking event with the intention and plan to meet new people.

If you have been at one of these events before, you are a step ahead. Either way, I can offer success strategies that will help make the most of your time at the event. Because remember, your time is valuable.

If you have never gone to a networking event before, does the idea of talking to strangers intimidate you? Does it give you anxiety? Make you want to run and hide? I mentioned this before, but now as you are thinking about facing a room full of strangers, please take comfort in knowing you are not alone in those feelings. To my shy or reluctant networking students, I say, "You told me you were working with me because you need to build your business. Do you want to be shy, or do you want to earn money? If you need customers, you can't have it both ways."

With some guidance from me and what you already have learned from this book, you will find that going to a networking event isn't as difficult as you might imagine. To those who are reluctant, I promise them that all they have to do is meet one new person. If they do that, they can go home. Most often, it turns out meeting just one new person is what makes them realize it isn't so difficult!

Let's start with your preparation.

Dress Appropriately.

Dress appropriately for the business you represent. If your business is a service or in a trade and you have uniformed apparel, that's fine as long as the clothing is fresh and clean. It can be a real bonus if your shirt is emblazoned with your logo. Otherwise, traditional business attire or business casual is fine, as long as you represent the business sector you work amongst.

Define Your Mission

Know whom you would like to meet. If you can preview the attendee list, choose at least two people you would like to meet. Don't forget the Anybody/Somebody rule. Look for target industries, companies or good referral sources for you. Choosing ahead of time gives you an advantage and a defined mission. When you meet someone on your list, tell them you've been wanting to meet them. They will be flattered.

Bring Plenty of Business Cards

You will be handing them out sparingly. More about that later.

Remember to be of Value First

Is there someone on the attendee list you can be of value to? It is easier to focus on helping others, and the pay-it-forward results are rewarding.

Don't Drink Alcohol

The danger in mixing alcohol and networking is being in the too-relaxed danger zone. Think of this as an extension of your workday— because it is. Go for the non-alcoholic beverages. You want to remain sharp and in control. Also, have some cash with you so you can tip appropriately. It's good business to tip, even if you only purchase a soda.

Practice Your Introduction

How should you introduce yourself? In all cases, make it short. "Hi, I'm Rob. "I teach people how to network." "Hi, I am Susan. I help business owners get more for their marketing dollar." That's it.

Plan to Arrive Early and Stay Late

I arrive at any networking event at least 30 minutes early and I stay a minimum of 30 minutes after it is officially over. I always have a cushion of time on either side. People think I'm nuts. I am not. Here is why.

If you arrive early, you are most likely to be the first person in the room. What's so good about that? You will be the first person to meet the second, third and fourth people who arrive. That means you will have met four new people before the event even starts!

Think of it like being the first person at a cocktail party. Please, forget the old adage about being fashionably late! That social custom has no place in business networking. One advantage of arriving early at a cocktail party is that you never have to feel self-conscious about walking into a room full of people who are already engaged in conversation. When you are the first to arrive, you can have one-on-one time to talk to the host, who notices you! You can observe the layout of the space, find the rest room, know what to do with your coat, and decide where the best vantage point might be. In fact, knowing where everything is makes you valuable to others who don't know.

In networking, it is much the same. When you arrive early, you meet the organizer who has seen your name on the registration. This is an opportunity for him or her to put a face to your name. You also have the opportunity to introduce yourself while he or she is not distracted, which helps to make you memorable. Always start this interaction with a compliment— express excitement for the event and appreciation for the opportunity to attend.

The people who run these events have great business connections, so it's big bonus to connect with them. The organizer also has the advantage of knowing who's who on the attendee list. If there is someone you want to meet, ask the organizer if that person is attending. If they are, ask them to introduce you during the event. If you feel self-conscious about asking, remember the organizer's goal is to make the event a success. Helping people make connections is part of that. Interacting with the organizer also makes you memorable. Always a plus!

Another benefit of arriving early is that most often the attendee name badges are arranged alphabetically on the registration table. Being early means you can visually scan all of them. When you don't have access to the attendee list ahead of time, this is a great advantage.

It's a very good practice to know what companies are sponsoring the event. Sometimes it is the organizer, but larger events are often sponsored by several organizations. If that is true, you should ask to meet the people who represent the sponsors.

The sponsors and the other people who arrive early are people who have built their businesses on strategically making the most of their time at the event. If you are there early, it is much easier to grab their attention and engage with them.

When you stay 30 minutes after the official end time, you can watch the

"Try and remember this phrase, 'If you're early - you're on-time, if you're on-time - you're late...and if you're late...don't bother!'"

crowd dissipate. You will learn to take notice of who left early. This sometimes indicates that that person has some importance in the business arena. If you missed him or her, make a note to catch up with them at the next event.

You will notice and be interested in the people who linger. Take it as an opportunity to engage with them in a more substantial conversation. My experience is that they are the ones who want to learn more about others and value the power of networking. As I mentioned before, people who share that value are people you want to find out more about. Try and remember this phrase, "If you're early - you're on-time, if you're on-time - you're late…and if you're late…don't bother!" Just my experience.

Name Badge Etiquette

Your name badge goes on the right side of your upper chest. Why? Because it works for both men and women, and because 95 percent of us are right-handed. Even if someone is left- handed, he or she shakes with the right hand. Positioning the name badge on your right just below your collarbone allows the other person to shake your hand, while it allows their eyes to travel your right arm to your shoulder to see your name. You should do the same. While you are shaking hands, you can easily see the name badge!

If you network regularly, you can have a magnetic name badge made with your name and logo. Be sure that your name is large enough to read easily.

Business Card Etiquette

There is only one business card rule. NEVER hand someone your business card unless the person asks for it. NEVER. Treat your business card like cash, as if each one was a dollar bill. If you go to a networking event for two hours would you give away $10 to $30 to random strangers? NO. It's not that you want to save money on printing more business cards. Rather, it is the same philosophy you would use in a financial investment. You only invest when you perceive value in doing so. Not papering the event in your business cards will also eliminate unwanted email solicitations from people who think having your email address is permission to add you to their mailing list. While we know that isn't supposed to happen, we know it does.

The reverse is also true. Don't ask for a person's card unless you intend to connect for a coffee chat after the event. Otherwise, you're wasting your time and are sending them a misleading message about your intentions.

"Treat your business card like cash"

You will meet people who give out their cards without being asked. They don't understand networking the way you do now. If they offer a card, accept it. There is no point in offending anyone. However, your time is valuable. Here is my suggestion for times when an unwanted business card is thrust upon you. After you accept the card, discretely fold it before you put it away in your pocket or purse. I repeat, discreetly. I simply put a fold in the corner of the card as I am putting it in my pocket. It is easy to do with your thumb. That way, when I am ready to add people to my contact list, I know the ones with the fold are of no interest to me.

Throwing them in the circular file saves me a lot of time! Welcome to being more efficient!

Look for Potential

Because you are meeting people for the first time, your goal is to try to discover if they seem like people you might want to learn more about. You are looking for potential candidates to include in your network. The F.O.R.M. rules apply, but you won't have time for all of that. You do want to start the conversation by asking questions first. You can use one or more of your F.O.R.M. questions. The ones I use most are the "Money" questions. Specifically, "Do you like what you do and/or when you attend an event like this Bob, who do you NEED to meet?" Again, it helps you learn if the person is committed to the current business.

If you don't like the answers, you don't have to worry about the rest of the conversation!

Break In or Break Free

As the room fills, you will see groups of two or more people clustered together talking. How do you break into an existing conversation? Or, do you? The answer depends on whether the group is "open" or "closed." Determining that is a matter of interpreting body language. If they stand close, leave no room between them, and are focused on each other, the group is closed, and you move on — with one exception: if one them is on your list of people to meet. If so, you can "hover." Stand a few feet outside of the group in view of the person you are targeting. Ideally, the person will notice you. You may even be able to make eye contact. That can signal that you are waiting to speak with him or her. Hopefully, the person will break with the circle or invite you in. The other option is to move on and keep the person in your sights until he or she is alone.

An open group will appear to be less intent in their conversation. The space between them will be wider. When you approach, others will notice you and yield a space to invite you in. This is a good thing for you to remember to do when you are in a group. Be aware of people around you and invite them into your conversation. It is the easiest way to meet new people without having to approach them, and it also is a great way to break free from a person or tedious conversation. The interruption is a graceful and easy opportunity to move on.

Remember, you are not at the event to get to know people in depth. Conversely, you aren't trying to meet everyone in the room, though most sales people will tell you it is all a numbers game— the more the better. With the RTM™ process, it isn't. It is meeting a few of the right people.

So, how else can you break free from a tedious conversation or someone who won't stop talking? There are three other ways: Pivot, Pass, and Pause.

"With the RTM™ process, it's meeting a few of the right people."

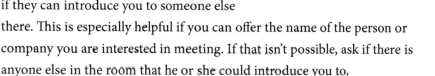

Pivot allows you to change or pivot the conversation by asking the other person if they can introduce you to someone else there. This is especially helpful if you can offer the name of the person or company you are interested in meeting. If that isn't possible, ask if there is anyone else in the room that he or she could introduce you to.

Pass is the second way to break into a conversation. Pass is pivoting in reverse. You pass the person on to someone else by offering to introduce him or her to someone you know or have just met. From there you can easily leave them to their conversation.

If those two don't work, a last resort is to use the Pause technique, which is to gracefully interrupt the conversation. Here are a few things you can say to do that. "I hate to interrupt you, but I am afraid I drank too much coffee and I need a bathroom break!" Then excuse yourself and leave quickly! Or, you could say, "Thanks so much. It's been great. But because we came here to meet new people, we probably should move on and do just that."

"With that, remind yourself to leave your ego at the door."

I will close this chapter with a cautionary note. I do this because we don't always realize our own behavior. I invite you to take a hard look at the attitude you show up with at events like this. Self-importance is never attractive. If you want to be highly successful, you examine your own conversation and behavior. With that, remind yourself to leave your ego at the door. Leave selling and sales aggression at the door. Confidence is wonderful, but show modesty.

Networking is not the time brag or be aggressive. We sell ourselves by behaving in a way that invites people to connect with us and like us. No one likes a blowhard. Enthusiasm and passion are admired, but a pushy braggart is to be avoided.

" ...the **biggest challenge** most networkers have... is **a failure to have a plan**."

CHAPTER
10

Networking at a Conference or Trade Show

Trade shows and conferences are great places to network. However, the biggest challenge most networkers have with them is a failure to have a plan. Their default plan is to walk around and talk to some of the vendors. The problem with that approach is that it wastes lots of time. So, have a plan.

What is the mantra about the value of your time? Right! "It's valuable, don't waste it."

Preparation

Remember, networking is an investment. Because it is time you aren't immediately compensated for, it makes it even more important to get results. It's not a willy-nilly exercise. Once again, advance research is where to start. Who will be there? What companies do you want to connect with? Who are the people you need to meet? What information sessions are going to be offered? Which topics, speakers or companies fit your target? How do you approach choosing workshops or seminars so you can make time for the sessions you want to attend? More about attending those sessions later.

As an example of targeting at an event like this, I recently went to a local chamber's business trade show. I was specifically looking for two things. One was for potential people to invite to my Networking In Diners® groups. For this, I was interested in insurance, banking and accounting professionals. I knew that I could find them in their booths.

My second focus was companies or organizations that would book me to speak. I chose companies, nonprofits and associations who might benefit from my ability to teach their people how to network by inviting them to a Lunch and Learn or other session.

These were my intentioned targets, you must define yours before you step foot in the hall.

Size Matters

The size of the trade show or conference matters. A huge event such as those held at the Javits Center in New York City, and other large venues means that you are faced with a sea of up to 1000 vendors to "swim" through. Simply walking the floor is impossible in one day, never mind stopping to chat. For those types of events, you must have a plan or you will come home with a bag full of business cards, useless marketing collateral and no real connections or prospects.

Start by researching the sponsors. The sponsors are spend large sums of money to make their presence known. They want to be noticed. They want to attract you and talk to you. They also can represent high-ticket sales for the right sale.

The rules are the same as those of networking events (remember the cocktail party analogy). You want to meet the host, in this case the organizer of the event. The organizers know all the insiders, VIP companies, and where all the businesses will be, and what they have planned for the show.

Now, I imagine you are wondering what to say when you find them. Simple. You say, "Hi! This is going to be a great show. Can you tell me, who are some of the most important people here today?"

You will discover that the host is going to mention the companies who are sponsoring the food, have planned expensive giveaways, or are giving a keynote speech or a highly topical seminar. Having that information allows you to be in the right places at the right times, so you can engage them.

No Selling!

Now you know who you need to meet, and before you hit the isles, here is the most important rule. You may recognize it. When you approach a booth, NEVER TRY TO SELL TO THE EXHIBITOR! Respect them, their investment, and mission. They are there to make sales contacts. Taking advantage of their time to promote your agenda is not how it works. In fact, it won't work— ever.

Another good reason to avoid that behavior is, most often, the people in the booth are not the people who are authorized to buy from you. Typically, they are salespeople. Their company is paying for the booth and for their time to staff the booth so they can obtain sales leads. Your conversational goal is to discover who in their organization is the right person for you to speak with. If the people in the booth happen to include the principal of the company or the person you should be speaking with, you will begin by not monopolizing their time with your spiel. You can ask for permission to contact them after the show.

Planning for Seminars and Speakers

Because seminars and speakers are promoted and scheduled in advance of the event, it's easy to make your plan for attending them. It's a good place to start because this information is most always available online before the event. If you start there, you know how to plan the time to approach your other targets.

If you are feeling apprehensive as you read this, let me share a conversation I recently had with a woman I am coaching. She is going to attend an international conference, and I am coaching her on how to navigate the conference. By the way, she's an introvert, so this whole scene is especially challenging for her. She says she does well with small bursts of extroverted energy, but it's limited, so her networking time is really valuable! To be successful, she must be focused and targeted.

Here's how our conversation went.

HER:

"So, here's the conference program. Rob, look at all the options. There are four tracks and two-day's worth of seminars!!! How do I do that?"

ME:

"Right. It's overwhelming. I know you are going to be there the night before the conference opens. You are certain to find the organizer buzzing around the conference floor. If not then, the next morning. When you do, say something as simple as, "Oh my gosh, there are so many different tracks and things in here, I just don't know what to choose from.""

That does two things. You get the organizer's attention, which means in order to give you suggestions, he or she must ask you about your business. BINGO. You give your two-sentence rollup about your business, why you are there, and what you're looking for. This way, he or she will be able to suggest a track, or at least a few seminars. Chances are the organizers know the presenters, too.

Just like the other meetings, there is a good chance, if you ask, the organizers will introduce you to the speaker before the seminar. If they don't, here's what you do. See if you can identify the speaker ahead of time. If you find the speaker, the ideal thing is to ask if he or she would have coffee with you. You could say, "[Organizer's name] said I should be sure to attend your seminar. I am so interested. Would you allow me to buy you a cup of coffee? I'd like to hear more about your topic."

Make sure you specify that you want to talk about the seminar topic, so the person doesn't think you have ulterior motives. This is important, because it is important to make it clear the conversation is for business purposes and nothing more. Coffee is the right choice. Offering a drink at the bar sends the wrong message regardless of the gender of the people involved.

HER:
"Yikes, approaching the speaker is scary! Why would they want to talk to me?"

ME:
"Chances are they may not agree, but they might! You don't know until you ask. If nothing else, they will remember you! Why? Because nobody does that. Why don't they? What is the one reason?"

HER:
"Well, I would find it difficult because I feel I would be bothering them. Who am I to ask for their time? I can't bother them! They are too busy."

M E :

"Right! Everyone is intimidated. The thing is, you never
ever can predict. You can never underestimate the value that
showing interest in someone else's business holds. Don't you
feel that way when someone asks you about yours?"

H E R :

"Well, yes, I do."

M E :

"If you were the one giving the presentation, how would you
feel if someone invited you to expound on it?"

H E R :

"I have to admit, I would be flattered."

M E :

"So, let's say you do a little of this reconnaissance. You try to
reach the host of the organizers and it doesn't happen. From
the program, you can find out who the sponsors are. Then you
peruse the program to see which seminars they are presenting.
You chose some you are interested in. From there, what would
be a good strategy?"

H E R :

"I don't know, don't be late for the seminar?"

ME:

"Yes, but there's more. If the reason for going to the seminar is more about meeting the speaker than the actual content, go early and see if you can snag a quick conversation with him/her. Sometimes, that person has a last minute need you can help with. Maybe the speaker needs a bottle of water or has a technical problem. You may not be able to fix it, but you could help by finding the person who could. You never know!

I was once at a seminar at a large conference. When the speaker left the room, she left her jacket on the chair. I noticed it, grabbed it and found her to return it. She was so grateful. We made a connection and I ended up getting a contract to work with her. That never would have happened if I hadn't talked with her that day".

HER:

"You are right, you just never know!"

ME:

"Here's another example. I wanted to talk with the organizer who was also giving a presentation. I was hoping that if I got there early enough I'd be able to grab him beforehand. I was successful in grabbing a selfie with him and that was it. It was perfect, because after he finished his presentation, he was completely barraged by 50 people. That went on for over an hour. I used the photo on my social media when I posted about the conference, which helped promote him. That made it easy to connect with him on social media afterwards, and I continue to cultivate that relationship."

HER:

"Okay, that makes sense. Actually, it practices what you always
say, too. First, my time is valuable. Why hang around and try
to compete with 50 people after a seminar if you can be the
only one before the seminar. Also, it allows you to continue
some type of relationship if you choose to."

ME:

"You got it! Okay, so when you go to the seminar,
where do you sit?"

HER:

"I always try to get as close to the front and
center as I can."

ME:

"WRONG!"

HER:

"Really? Don't I want them to notice me?"

ME:

"No. Because they won't anyway. Not unless you do something
weird or awful while they are presenting. The reason to sit in
the back at any seminar is what if the presentation if awful, or
you really need a bathroom break, or you need to take a call or
meet someone? If you are in the back, near the door, you can
slip out without causing an embarrassing disruption for you or
the speaker."

HER:

"Yeah, and if the presentation really is bad, you are not a prisoner, stuck there wasting your time!"

ME:

"Right! I always sit in the back for that reason. Also, it makes it easy to watch how the rest of the attendees are reacting. Sometimes what an attendee says triggers me to realize I might want to connect with others in the audience, too. From where I am sitting, I can intercept them on their way out.

If I do stay to connect with the speaker, I say, "I really enjoyed that very much." Then the coup de grâce is asking him or her to them to grab coffee with me right then. Unless the person has to go right to a book signing or other commitment, he or she could probably use a break. Engaging with the speaker can be the perfect situation if they accept. Most of the time the answer will be something such as, "Mmm no, I can't." I have gotten a "Yes." It is challenging, though. It does make you a gold-level-networker if you can do it. If you succeed, you have my permission to go home, put up your feet and celebrate, because you did it!"

HER:

"So, what happened the first time you were gold-level successful? What was that like?"

ME:

"Honestly, I was caught off guard. When he accepted my invitation, I had no idea what to do. So, I bought us coffee and I fell back on my default question, which is tell me, how did you get started in doing what you're doing now?"

HER:

"Great question."

ME:

"Yes, it is a good one. It is always a good conversation starter.
Most people will talk for at least five minutes about their
professional history. From there, I had time to know where I
wanted to take the conversation.

HER:

"I am thinking that people...the person that you're
asking feels more at ease if they are sure you're not
trying to pitch them something."

ME:

"Exactly."

HER:

"It would be smart to say something at the moment
you invite them for coffee that would convey that.
Maybe, can I buy you coffee? I would be interested in
knowing more about why you do what you do, and
how you got to this point in your career."

ME:

"Good idea. I always say, how can we help
each other in business? I like to make it
clear that the interest is not personal, so
they realize I have no hidden agenda."

HER:

"Smart."

Walking the Show Floor

HER:

"Okay, that's targeting specific people and getting them to engage with me. What about the rest of the show, the rest of the booths and people? Do I just ignore them?"

ME:

"No! You still have your list of exhibitors that you want to meet."

HER:

"I know who I am targeting and I am not supposed to approach them with my spiel, so when I go to the booth what do I do? Do I just wait for them to ask me questions?"

ME:

"No, you can say, so, why are you exhibiting here today?"

HER:

"And they say, "Because my boss sent me here, right?"

ME:

"Not necessarily. They may give you that quizzical, tilted-head look that your dog gives you sometimes when it is puzzled, but more often you will hear something like, 'because we belong to the association and we wanted to make sure we supported them.' That's code for, we need business. The people I want to talk to are the ones who come right out and say they need more sales. Now you can bypass the rapport and go right to, 'Tell me about that.'

So, that's what I suggest for attending a trade show or conference. Do you have any other questions?"

HER:

"Yes. Let's say that it isn't a local trade show or conference. You traveled there and the vendors are from all over the country or globe. Unless I do it at the show, I'm not going to be able to sit down and have coffee with them because we're all going to go our separate ways.

Right? So, then what?"

ME:

"You ask for their business card first, because you determined there was something about the connection that is worth following up on. Remember that if they have traveled to the show, they're staying at a hotel somewhere nearby. You could invite them to have dinner with you. Be aware that doing this can be tricky, because they may think your interest is more personal.

Asking them to have coffee is better. You can say, I don't know if you get any breaks. If so, maybe we can have a coffee and talk more about your company."

HER:

"And if not then, what? Do I go home and just send an email or ask for a connection on LinkedIn? Do we ever have a conversation?"

"You ask for their business card first, because you determined there was something about the connection that is worth following up on."

M E :

"Well, if you can't meet with them during the show, then
you ask for permission to call them after the show. Then you
do a follow-up phone conversation or email conversation.

You've already done all the rapport, so you can remind them
that they gave you permission and say, I don't want to take
up a lot of your time. I really enjoyed connecting with you
at the show and you gave me permission to call you. Might
you be able to introduce me to the person who handles . . .?"

H E R :

"Yes, that's not so difficult, because they gave
you the permission."

M E :

"Also, if it makes sense for your business, you could ask
if their company has a branch in your home state or
within some drivable distance. They could connect you to
someone there."

Exhibiting and Networking

H E R :

"Okay now, so let's reverse the role. What about if I am
an exhibitor and you come to my booth and ask me why
I am exhibiting. What do I say?"

M E :

"You say, Because, of course, I want more clients. This is a
good way to promote my business and my brand. Exhibiting
is a great way to do that. What is it that you do?

If you are the first to engage them from your booth, you
say, Hi, what brings you to the show today? Regardless of
what side of the event you are on, you want to be succinct.
Ask questions to make it a productive conversation. What
often happens is the person attending the trade show goes
to the exhibitors and tries to sell them. The person who
is exhibiting at that booth begins to counter with selling
as well. They're both trying to figure out how to make the
puzzle piece fit. It rarely happens because the conversation
got off on the wrong foot."

HER:

"Do you expect an indication for the puzzle piece to fit by
the time you're done with that conversation, on either side
of the table?"

ME:

"The intention is to make the puzzle pieces fit. One essential
piece in making it fit is if the other person does the Organic
Switch. It's when the other person asks you questions.
It's the natural reciprocity I mentioned before. It usually
happens with people who are interested in creating business
relationships. If it doesn't happen, you have a decision
to make. Often, it means it's time to move on. If it does
happen, just like in the coffee chat, it starts the process of
discovering the potential to connect further. If the person is
selling dog collars and your business is snake oil, maybe the
pieces don't fit, but you both target pet store owners! You
decide the value and see if they do, too. Follow the plan, and
keep going!"

Exhibiting Do's & Don'ts

If you are exhibiting at a show or conference, here are some suggestions that can help you be successful.

- Always go early to set up.

- Go early before the show opens to network with those in the other booths.

- Never ever sit down in your booth.

- Never ever sit behind a table.

- Never ever have a table!

- If necessary, use a short cocktail table with a draped skirt.

- If you have to have a table for show displays or collateral, put the table back against the wall or curtain.

- Don't leave giveaways out for everyone to grab. You might even want to have more expensive, selective giveaways that you offer only when the Organic Switch happens.

- Put mints on the table and in your pocket.

- Have a raffle item and bowl for them to place their card in.

- Wear your name tag. It's best to purchase a magnetic one ahead of time that has your name and logo on it. Remember, on your right side!

- Curb your coffee intake…try anyway.

- Drink plenty of water because you will be shocked at how fast your body will dehydrate standing in a booth.

- Stay away from unhealthy snacks.

- Bring your own healthy snacks: fruit and nuts or energy bars.

- Don't eat in your booth. It's okay to pop a mint or piece of snack food in your mouth when no one is there, or leave the booth for your snack time.

Finally, big conferences often have cocktail parties and dinner events. Remember, it's club soda all the way for you. Many people don't want to hear that. However, this is work. It's not time to relax. Things can go in the wrong direction very quickly when alcohol is involved. Be smart, stick with the basic networking event rules.

❝ After reading this book, you are officially "on notice!" **YOU are the better Networker now...YOU follow-up!"**

CHAPTER
11

After the Networking Event

No matter the event, a seminar, a leads group meeting, a networking event, or visiting or exhibiting at a trade show, your post-event follow-up is critical to the process of successful networking. It's important that your follow-up is timely. If you are fortunate, the other person will follow-up with you, but you can't trust or wait for that to happen. Unless you take responsibility and action, you can't begin to make anything happen. After reading this book, you are officially "on notice!" YOU are the better Networker now...YOU follow-up!

Follow-up Begins Immediately

Follow-up begins IMMEDIATELY following the event, and I mean immediately. As soon as the event ends, you need to sit and make notes on each card before your memory fades and you lose the inspiration and momentum. I actually take a few minutes in the car before I leave the parking lot. What helps is that you partially prepared during the event. Remember, I told you when you take someone's business card, you make a choice then and there whether or not you see value in setting up a meeting with that person. If you don't see value, you fold the card as you put it away. As you prepare to follow-up with your desired contacts, you have already categorized at the first level and taken charge by being selective with your time and your attention. You don't bother with the folded cards, because you value your time and you don't waste it.

"If you wait, and don't follow-up... I promise you, I GUARANTEE YOU, all your networking will be wasted time and energy."

On the business cards of the people you deemed to be good connections, you need to write a quick note on the card. Even in this day of technology, you should always have a pen! Keep a few in your car if you don't want to carry one. If you don't have one, you can resort to taking notes on your phone, but that makes it more difficult later. The note you write is to remind you of your intention or reason for wanting to follow-up with that person. It's a good idea to note the date and/or the event on the card. That way, if you happen to misplace the card and find it later, the information will allow you to check back on your event calendar to help you remember more about the connection.

If you had already discussed a plan to set up a date to meet for coffee or a meal, write that down. A simple code like C4C (connect for coffee) can be your shorthand reminder. Perhaps, the person promised to invite you to another event or group, or to introduce you to someone in his or her circle of contacts. Write it down. You can make up your own shorthand if you like.

What other kinds of notes would you typically make? If you promised to connect them to another one of your contacts, write down your contacts name on the card so you remember to make the connection.

As you become more comfortable with networking and this process of making notes, you can even make notes right in front of the person. You can simply explain that you do it so that you won't forget what the two of you discussed. They will be flattered.

The important thing to be aware of is how quickly your memory will fade, even as quickly as the next day, especially if you do a fair amount of networking. If you wait, and don't follow-up in a timely fashion, I promise you, I GUARANTEE YOU, all your networking will be wasted time and energy. The priority for following up and the memory of why you intended to will keep your momentum and energy flowing.

The 48-Hour Rule

The next thing you need to do is go to LinkedIn and invite these new connections to connect with you. Do this within 48 hours, so that the memory of meeting at the event is still fresh in their minds, too. I am a firm believer in the value of LinkedIn. It not only is the best online tool for making and keeping contacts, it is also a turnkey resource for RTM™ networking.

Again, this is where nearly everyone fails. We all become too busy and forget the value we defined when we met the person. The standard is to connect with him or her no more than 48 hours after the event, and then 48 hours after the person responds back to you. This time-sensitive practice is all about staying in the forefront of people's minds, and keeping their intention and interest in you active as well.

If the person accepts your LinkedIn invitation, send them a message through LinkedIn. Do it as soon as possible. If your follow-up involves a meeting the messages should read, "Thanks so much for connecting with me. I look forward to getting together for breakfast, lunch or coffee, to see how we can help each other in business."

I recently met a women who was newly hired as the director of corporate strategy for her company. Our initial conversation told me she could be a good connection. For some reason, which I will ask when I actually have coffee with her, I couldn't find her on LinkedIn. The point is that it is important to be where people can find you, and where you can connect easily and strategically with the largest number of people in your target market. In her case, I will send an email to connect with her again.

Other Social Media

Should you limit making connections only via LinkedIn? The answer is, no! If you are on other social media platforms, you should connect with your contacts. Contacts that you feel mutually comfortable connecting with are valuable. Some platforms offer different profiles, pages or feeds for both personal and business. Connecting on social media makes it easy to get a sense of a person's likes, dislikes and opinions. You discover what he or she does with leisure time. In a way, connecting on social media offers an easy way to discover some of the personal information you seek in the F.O.R.M. process. For instance, I 1discovered that one of my connections was really into Civil War History. So am I. That makes for a much warmer connection when I meet with him.

A note of caution. It is a good idea to remember that if someone posts something that could be considered controversial, it doesn't mean we have to react or respond. I believe there are subjects and opinions that are best left alone on social media…or in general for that matter. If you encounter those types of posts (religious or political as examples), it is best not to react or respond at all. As an open channel of opinion, social media is valuable, but it can also be a slippery slope.

When it comes to communication outside of LinkedIn, my default is email communication to set up appointments. I like it because, like LinkedIn, it is a form of documentation. My second choice is a phone call. My own personal rule, yours could be different, is that I don't text a contact unless I have gotten specific permission from them to do so. I do not care if people choose to text me. In fact, I will often mention that the number on my business card is my mobile number and say it's okay to text me. Just remember if you text anyone that you've only just met, you may not be in their contact list. It's a good idea to include your name at the beginning of the first text you send to them.

Third-party Connections

If I am on the receiving end of a virtual introduction or connection from one of my contacts, it usually comes by email. The 48-hour rule still applies. I prefer to do it immediately upon receiving the email. I simply shoot off a quick reply that reads, "Nice to meet you virtually. I look forward to meeting you in person over breakfast, lunch or coffee." Then, I wait to see what happens. I do still go to LinkedIn to make the connection there.

When I virtually connect people, I do it through my LincSphere account. It makes it easy to connect people and send a short 160-character note such as, "You have a lot in common, you should connect."

Of course, both people have to be in my LincSphere contact list. I update it as needed, but review the contacts about once a month or once a quarter.

One thing that can be tricky is requesting that people connect you with one of their connections, especially if the person you are wanting to meet is a high-profile person. Let's say we've just met at a chamber event and Bob tells me that he knows Jack Welch. I really want to connect with him. That is valuable information for me, and I don't want to lose the connection. In that case, I send an email message first that reads, "Hi Bob, if it's okay, I will connect with you on LinkedIn." As that connection process continues and transforms, we will meet. When we do, I will mention to Bob what he told me about knowing Jack Welch and ask to hear the story. I won't ask at that time to be connected, but I might say something like, "Someday I might ask you to connect me to him. How would that work?"

In a case like that one, Bob's story and the response to the connection question should indicate the validity of his relationship with Jack Welch. If it is real, my strategy for becoming connected goes beyond typical networking. I understand the value of his relationship and I honor it by taking time to build one with him that is authentic and meaningful to him as well. That involves trust, which takes time.

Often, I am asked about how far I will travel to have coffee with a connection. It only takes 90 minutes to get anywhere in Connecticut, depending on traffic, of course. I will drive that far or farther, because I have already determined there is value in it. I do try to combine meetings in a geographic area to make my travel worthwhile. Your own type of business and ability to serve customers outside of your geographic area will dictate how far you will travel.

Within 48 hours of your networking event, your coffee meeting preparation begins a new cycle with the RTM™ process of networking.

"Networking is not just for salespeople and business owners. **Employees can benefit from networking** within their organizations."

CHAPTER 12

Networking from Within Your Organization

Networking is not just for salespeople and business owners. Employees can benefit from networking within their organizations. In fact, doing so can be as important to the success of an employee's career as it is to the success of a business.

My method offers actionable strategies that are applicable to networking within an organization, too. In that case, your colleagues, co-workers, and your superiors in the hierarchies of organizations are the contacts you want to make connections with. My strategies can be applied in all of those relationships. Regardless of whether it's internal or external networking, the evergreen questions are, "What do you wish to accomplish and who do you need to meet?"

Jeff's Story

Jeff is the person who assisted me a few years ago in obtaining the opportunity to present my RTM™ networking training to Pepsi. I feel a special bond with him because he's a fellow Eagle Scout. That last piece of information keeps him high on my list because I know that our value systems come from the same tribe.

Jeff is a 25-year veteran of corporate America. When I met him, he was working for a large well-known corporation, having advanced within by working hard and earning a good reputation. Jeff has never been self-employed or owned a business. He has never been to a chamber of commerce meeting. He has never had to do the kind of outreach entrepreneurs or business owners have to do to find clients for his business or earn a paycheck, and he is not a salesperson for his company. What he does have to do within his company is "play nice" with his co-workers, and sell himself and his ideas to his superiors. Like many in his world, he also is very interested in moving up the ladder of success within his company.

One evening, Jeff and I had dinner. He was excited to tell me he'd gotten a new job. I said, "Great! So, tell me, where do you fit in the organization?" He immediately grabbed a handful of sugar packets and started laying out the organizational chart with the packets. I thought it was such a clever way to define the chart. I could easily see where he fit in and why.

His new job was for a subsidiary of his former company. Even though the two companies are related, their cultures are totally different. For Jeff, that was like starting over. He assumed that in his new position his history would follow him. While his credentials and experience did, his relationships did not. In the new company, he was as unknown as any new employee. He hadn't realized that he wasn't going to be able to rely on old allies. In the new job, this meant there was no one in the hierarchy that could help him continue to grow.

The problem that Jeff was facing was that his new job was also a new position that resulted from recent reorganization. Actually, he had had his site set on a job that was two sugar packet rows above his, but he couldn't figure out how to get to it.

My question as I pointed to his own sugar packet was, "If you're down here and you want to get up two levels, do you know all of the people in the row just above you?"

"No," he said. "I know one of them, maybe two of them but I don't know all three, and none of them know me."

"Ah," I said. "Well you know they all know each other really well, right?"

At that point, he froze for a moment and said, "Well no, why? How would you know that?"

"Because," I said, "They're all at the same level. They're all directors. That's how they know each other."

"Really?" he said.

"Yes, that's how they all know each other. And by the way, they probably play golf together and even go out to eat together, because they're all at the same level."

"Well I don't do that with the people who are on my level," he said.

Jeff can definitely benefit from knowing how to do what I call, Networking Over The Wall, which is strategically cultivating relationships over the real and invisible walls that divide those in the corporate world. It's networking from within, because success in the corporate world is still very much about connections and influence. It is about whom you know, and more so about who knows you, why they know you, what they know about you, and also their influence in the organizational hierarchy.

I told Jeff he should cultivate relationships on his level, even do it socially. And he needed to focus on making inroads with those who could connect him to the people at the top of the organization. That would require him to network within the organization. But how?

His challenge was to find out about the people above him. Not simply their names and titles, but their roles and influence. I told him he needed to meet with them. If this is your challenge, too, you need to remember a few key things.

First, start by networking with your co-workers. Engaging them over time with F.O.R.M. questions is the easiest way. Very often, co-workers offer valuable information about others, including those in positions of authority. Creating good connections at your own level is essential to your accomplishments.

Second, as you embark on networking with higher levels in the organization, remember those people know each other well. What you say to one will surely be common knowledge to all. There are no secrets. Always remember that!

"One thing all management and executives value is employees who are interested in the company and engaged in it."

Third, you need to understand the culture of the organization. If management subscribes to an open-door policy, it will be easier to engage with superiors. If not, you will need to be strategic and aware of ways and opportunities to engage with them.

The corporate environment is a closed ecosystem. Knowing the players is both easier and more difficult than networking outside of it, because your access to the upper echelon is likely somewhat restricted. You are not often on the same playing field. That calls for more of a strategy than networking outside of employment.

You probably won't be able to walk into the office of a person two levels above you to ask him or her to have coffee with you! You probably don't have a lot of contact with most of those people, but perhaps you can look for opportunities in the hallway, elevator, cafeteria, or before or after a meeting. At those intersections, everyone is basically on the same level because you're engaged in the same activity, which makes conversation easier.

Then you just have to do it. You have to talk to them.

One thing all management and executives value is employees who are interested in the company and engaged in it. Saying something such as, "I wonder if I could have a few minutes of your time, maybe grab a cup of coffee or meet for lunch. I really wanted to meet you and understand more about the vision of the company and your role. I am also interested in how I can contribute more effectively."

What you want them to think is, "Now, here's somebody who is really interested in this company."

I know that approaching someone that way sounds so scary. However, the number one reason Pepsi brought me in to train its staff is it values its people and wants to invest them. The cost to hire and to train a new employee is substantial. Believe me, the company wants to keep the employees it has.

"Fear is the number one killer of dreams and successful networking!"

I taught Pepsi employees how to ask the right questions to advance their careers and how to identify whom they needed to be asking. The reason people don't is because they're afraid. Fear is the number one killer of dreams and successful networking! If I had let fear overcome me, I would never have had lunch with Roger, my executive vice president contact, in the first place. Was I apprehensive, even out and out scared? I was, but I invited him to lunch anyway. The fact he said yes scared me even more! It didn't stop me though.

In his new position, Jeff's biggest problem is that he really wants to work for someone he doesn't know in the organization. His ultimate goal is to work in another segment of the business for someone whose reputation he admires. He knows exactly who he wants to meet! I told him, "Okay, Jeff, you just need to go over and ask him for a breakfast, lunch or coffee! Because, if this person doesn't get to know you, how do you have any hope of getting where you want to go?"

So, Jeff, where is the closest diner?

ABOUT ROB THOMAS

Rob Thomas is a master of business development having an 20-year career of growing and managing regional territories for Iron Mountain, Aflac and the Greater New Haven, CT Chamber of Commerce, just to name a few.

Rob credits his success to his own brand of networking, which turns the adage, "It's not what you know, but who you know," into a new and actionable process.

Today, as a business entrepreneur and creator of the *Rob Thomas Method*™ of Networking, Rob teaches and coaches business owners and sales people on how to grow business by identifying and building a network of effective relationships.

Rob also works with large organizations from C-level executives on down. He helps them employ the *Rob Thomas Method*™ as their internal networking process, to build stronger relationships and add value within the organization.

One more personal things about Rob, you might never otherwise know, he is a Mason and played clarinet in High school!

Made in the USA
Middletown, DE
03 April 2019